CHRISTMAS BOOK

LEVEL 4

T0086934

PIANO
Adventures®
by Nancy and Randall Faber
THE BASIC PIANO METHOD

CONTENTS

About the "Sightreading Stocking Stuffers"

A student's enthusiasm for learning Christmas music can become an opportunity to create enthusiasm for sightreading. In this book, each Christmas song is presented with short melodies, called "Sightreading Stocking Stuffers."

The "Sightreading Stocking Stuffers" are inspired by the carol being studied. Through repetition of familiar rhythmic, melodic, and harmonic patterns, the student builds a visual and aural musical vocabulary.

The "stocking stuffers" provide opportunity for transposition, reinforcing theory and musicianship skills.

The student should sightread one "stocking stuffer" a day while learning the Christmas song. Or, the stocking stuffers can be used as sightreading during the lesson itself.

The teacher may wish to tell the student:

> **Sightreading means "reading music at first sight."**
> When sightreading, music is not practiced over and over. Instead, it is only played several times with the highest concentration.

The following **3 C's** may help the student with sightreading:

CORRECT HAND POSITION
Find the correct starting note for each hand. Scan the music for rhythmic and melodic patterns. Look for any hand position changes before starting to play!

COUNT - OFF
Set a steady tempo by counting one "free" measure before starting to play.

CONCENTRATE
Focus your eyes on the music, carefully reading the intervals. Remember to keep your eyes moving ahead!

FF1142

Note to Teacher: This page reviews time signatures and rhythms, preparing the student for the carols and sightreading that follow.

Stuffing the Stockings

Draw a line connecting the rhythm in each gift to the correct stocking (time signature).

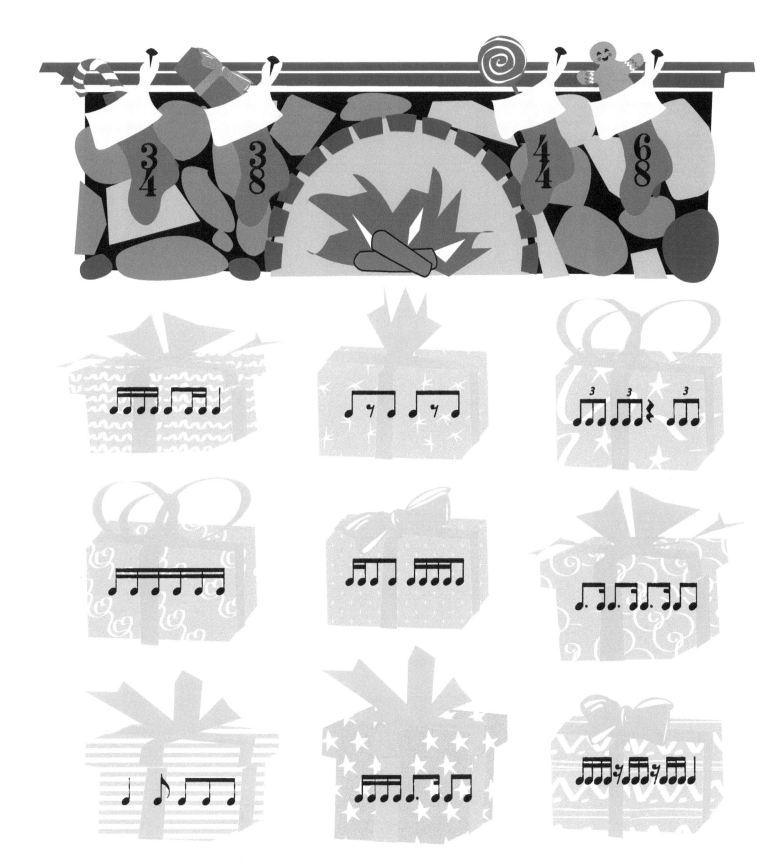

Extra Credit: Your teacher may ask you to play each rhythm on the piano using a major or minor chord of your choice.

It Came Upon the Midnight Clear

E.H. Sears and R.S. Willis

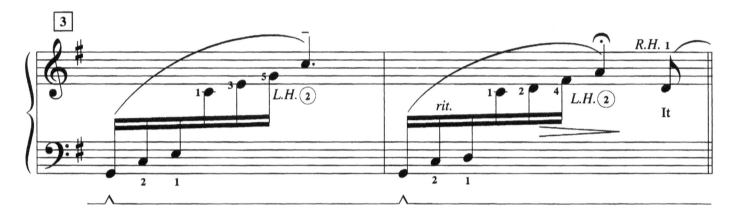

FF1142

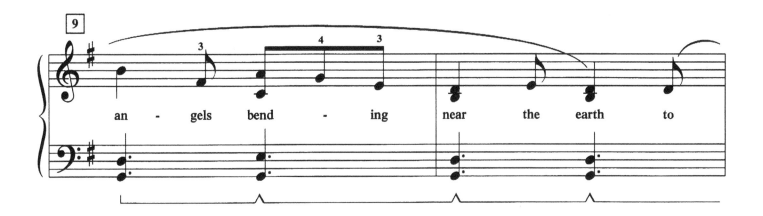

an - gels bend - ing near the earth to

touch their harps_____ of gold._____ *f* "Peace

on the earth_____ good - will to men, from

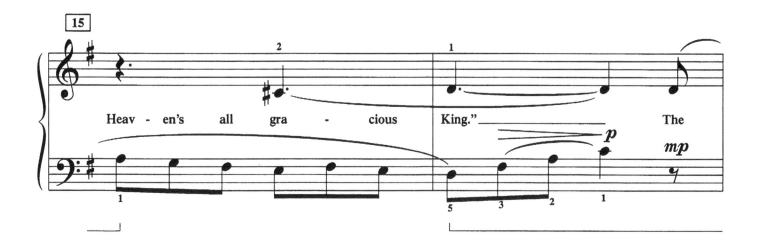

Heav - en's all gra - cious King."_____ *p* *mp* The

world in sol - emn still - ness lay to

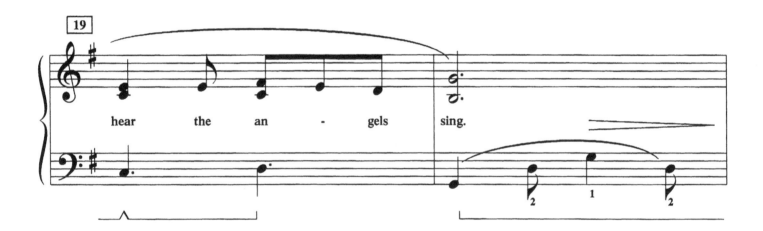

hear the an - gels sing.

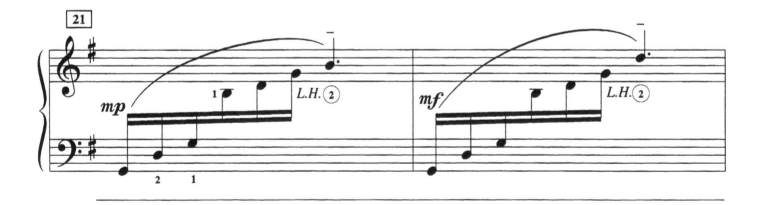

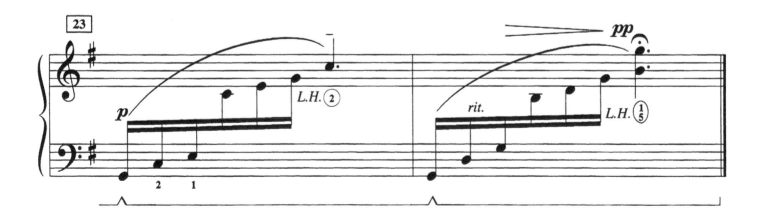

Sightread one "stocking stuffer" a day while learning *It Came Upon the Midnight Clear.*

Circle the stocking after sightreading!

("variations" for sightreading)

Circle the 6ths before sightreading.

Circle the 6th before sightreading.

Circle the 6ths before sightreading.

Circle the 6th before sightreading.

DAY 5

In the carol, put a ✔ above each measure with this rhythm:

Hint: There are 5.

DAY 6

Transpose **Day 1** to F major.

Hint: First play as written in G.
Then transpose **down a step** to F major.
(R.H. begins on C, the dominant note.)

Housetop Boogie

Words and Music by
Benjamin Russell Hanby

Moderately (without swing rhythm)

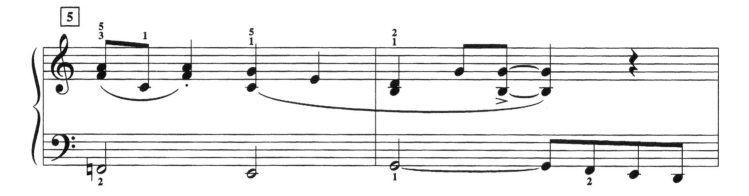

FF1142

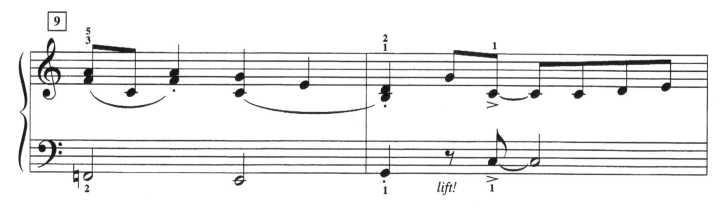

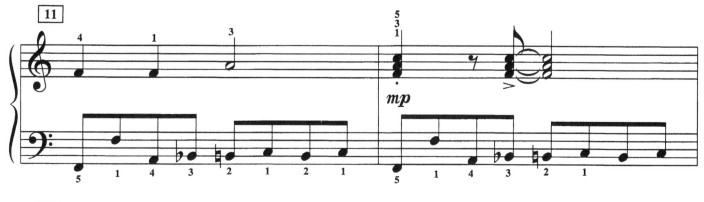

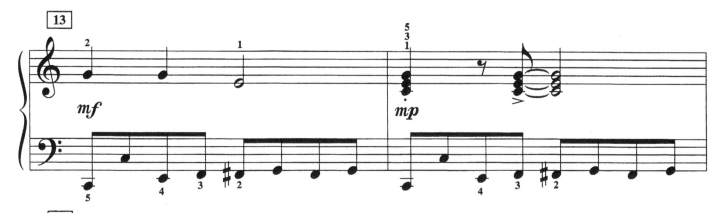

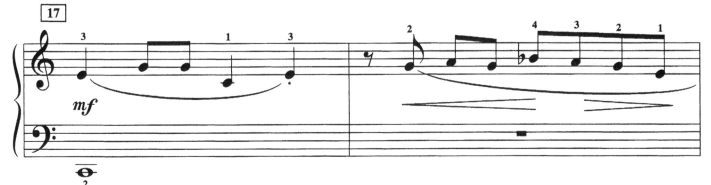

FF1142

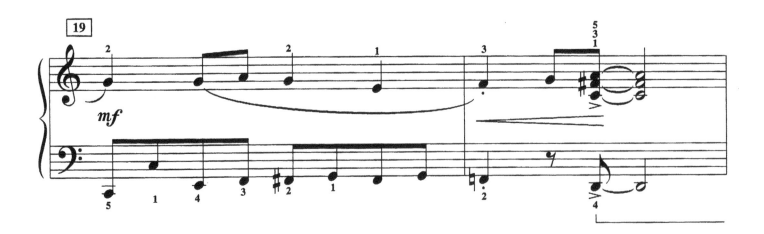

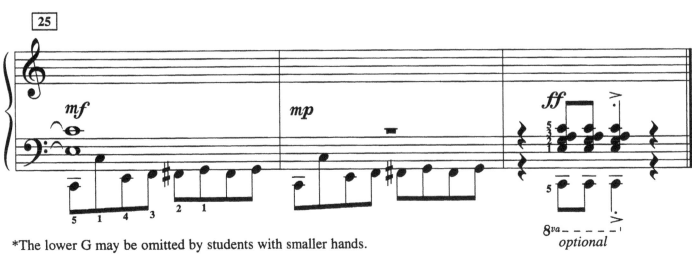

*The lower G may be omitted by students with smaller hands.

FF1142

Sightread one "stocking stuffer" a day
while learning *Housetop Boogie.*

Circle the stocking after sightreading!

BOOGIE WOOGIE STOCKING STUFFERS

("variations" for sightreading)

Can you transpose to G major?

DAY 1

DAY 2

Can you transpose to F major?

DAY 3

Look for hand position changes before sightreading.

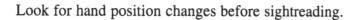

DAY 4

DAY 5   Which stocking stuffer uses *imitation* between the hands? **Day** ___

DAY 6   Which stocking stuffer uses pattern and *sequence*? **Day** ___

Silent Night

Words by Joseph Mohr
Music by Franz Grüber

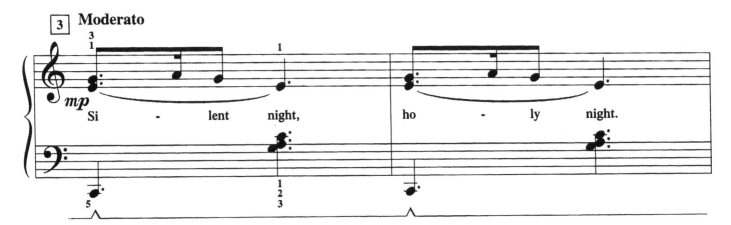

Si - lent night, ho - ly night.

All is calm, all is bright

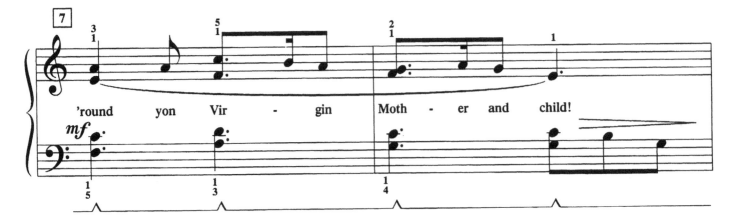

'round yon Vir - gin Moth - er and child!

Ho - ly In - fant so ten - der and mild,

Sleep in heav - en - ly peace,_____

poco rit.

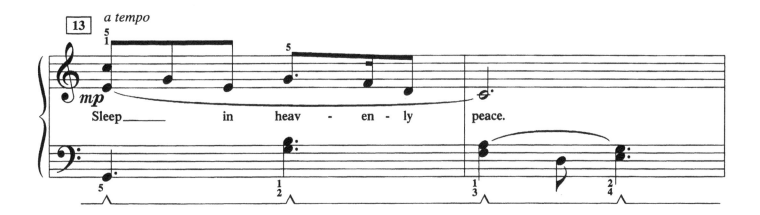

Sleep_____ in heav - en - ly peace.

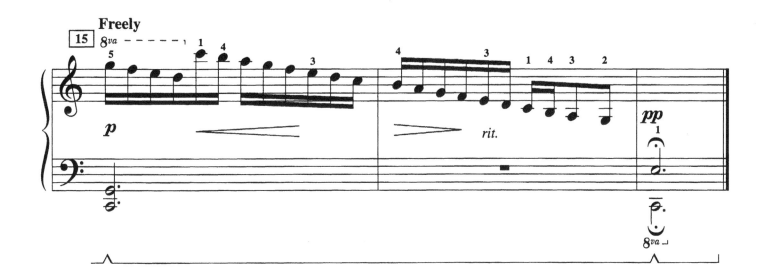

Sightread one "stocking stuffer" a day while learning *Silent Night.*

Circle the stocking after sightreading!

("variations" for sightreading)

Can you transpose to G major?

DAY 5 In *Silent Night*, write the counts *1 2 3 4 5 6* under the correct beats for the first 2 measures.

DAY 6 In *Silent Night*, put a ✔ above each measure with this rhythm:

Ave Maria

Bach-Gounod

Andante

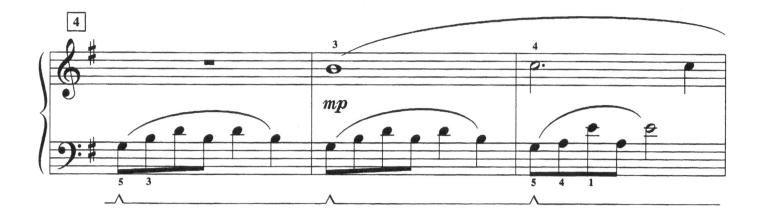

pedal simile

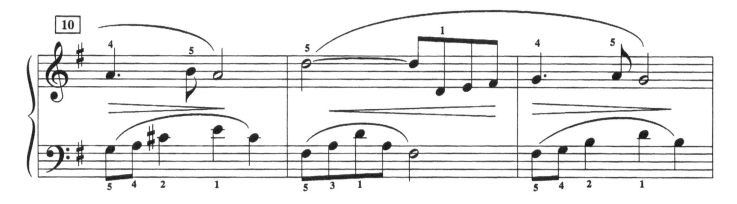

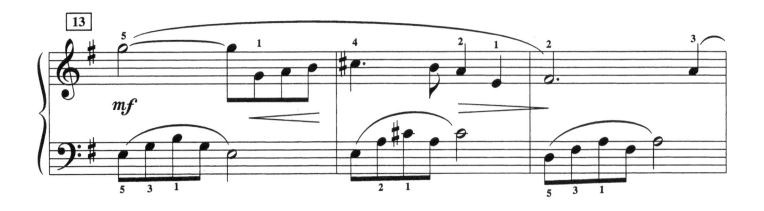

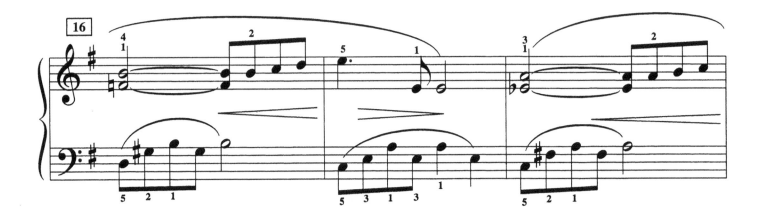

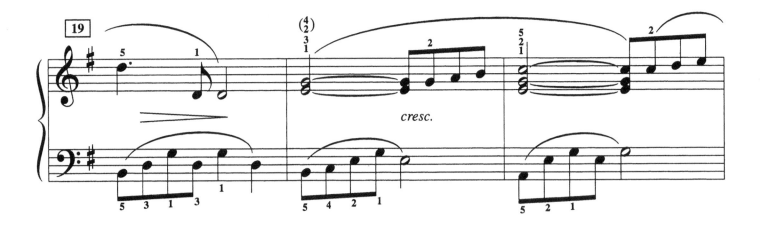

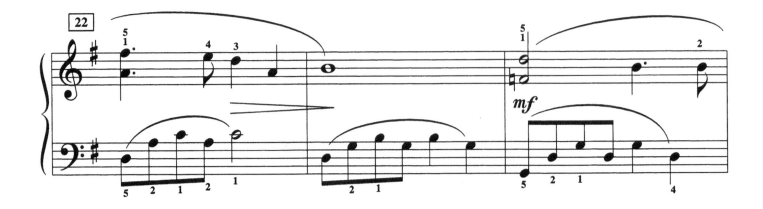

cresc. poco a poco

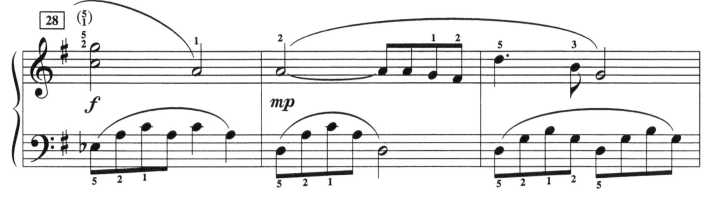

f *mp*

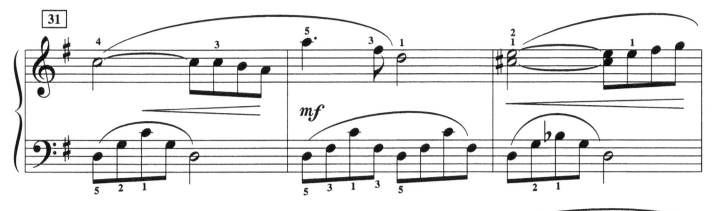

mf

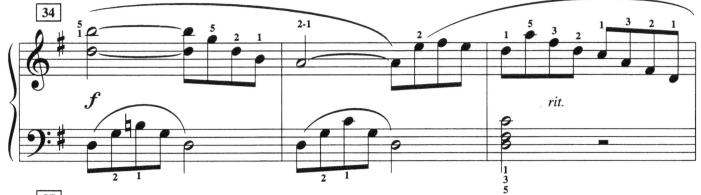

f *rit.*

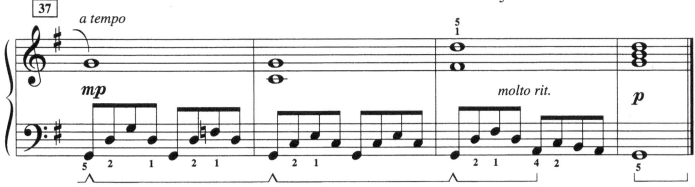

a tempo

mp *molto rit.* *p*

Sightread one "stocking stuffer" a day
while learning *Ave Maria.*

Circle the stocking after sightreading!

("variations" for sightreading)

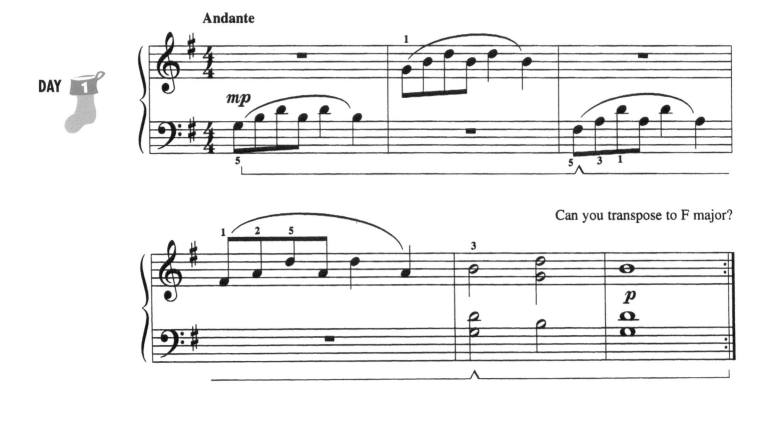

DAY 1

Andante

mp

Can you transpose to F major?

p

DAY 2

Andante

mp

mf

Can you transpose to C major?

FF1142

DAY 3

DAY 4

DAY 5

Label the harmony for each measure of **Day 1** as a G or D major chord.

(Write **G** or **D** above each measure.)

DAY 6

In *Ave Maria*, put a ✔ above each measure with this rhythm:

Waltz of the Flowers
(from *The Nutcracker Suite*)

Peter Ilyich Tchaikovsky

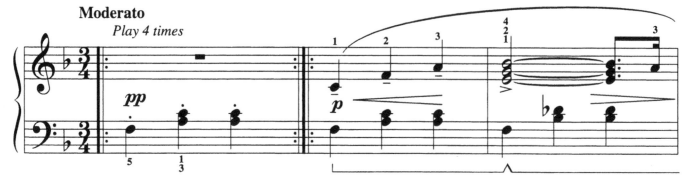

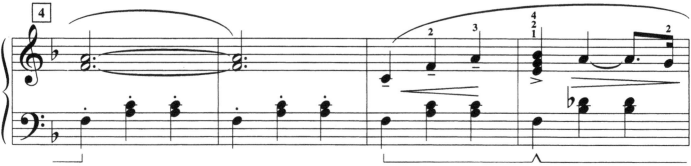

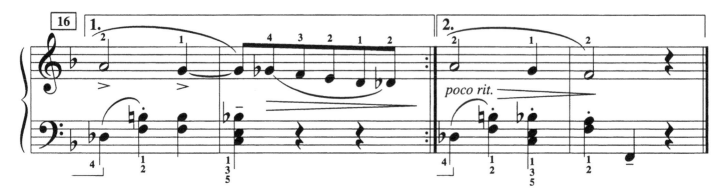

20

Sightread one "stocking stuffer" a day
while learning *Waltz of the Flowers.*

Circle the stocking after sightreading!

("variations" for sightreading)

Can you transpose to G major?

DAY **1**

Can you transpose to C major?

DAY **2**

Can you transpose to D major?

DAY **3**

Can you transpose to C major?

DAY **4**

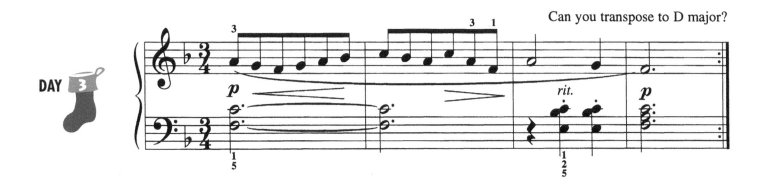

DAY **5**

In *Waltz of the Flowers,* which
measure has a **1st inversion**
C major chord for the L.H.?

measure ____

DAY **6**

In *Waltz of the Flowers,* which measure
has a **1st inversion** G minor chord for
the L.H.? measure ____

Can you find a **2nd inversion** G minor
chord for the L.H.? measure ____

FF1142

21

Take a trip through music history with each rendition of this Christmas favorite.
Can you "travel" from the Baroque to the present before Christmas arrives?

We Wish You a Merry Christmas
(A Christmas Tour through Music History)

At a Baroque Christmas Party (1600-1750)

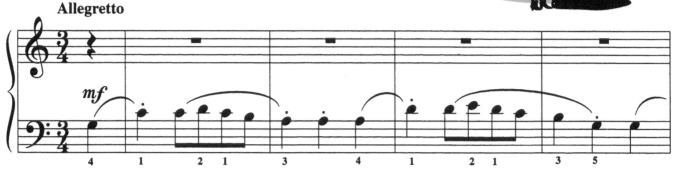

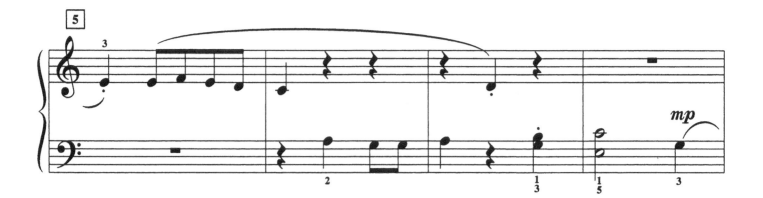

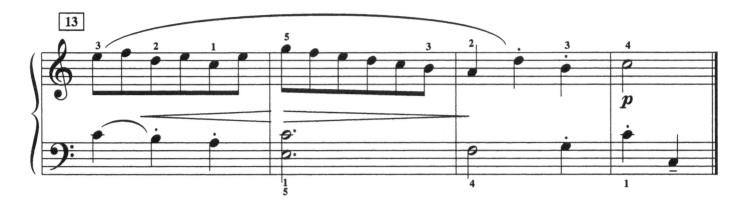

FF1142

At a Classical Party (1750-1830)

Moderato

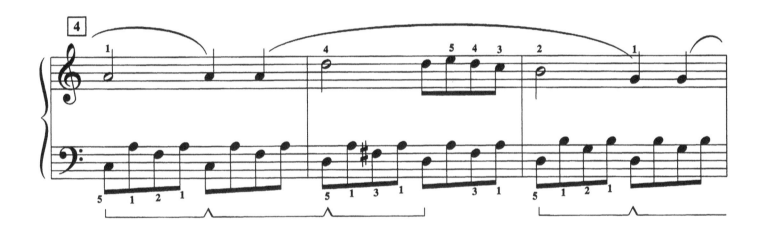

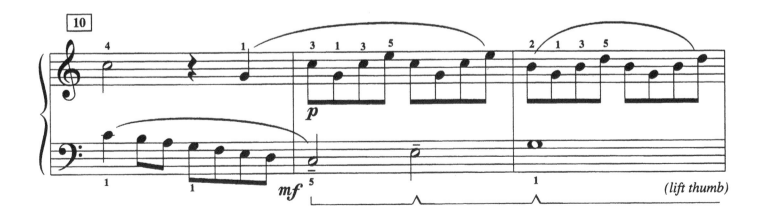

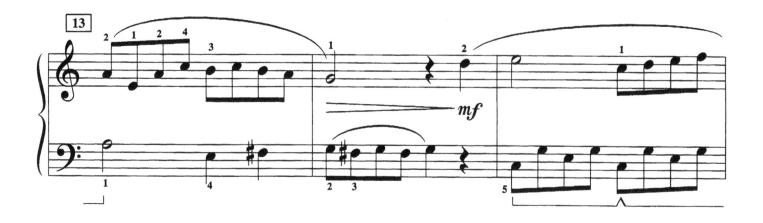

At a Romantic Christmas Party (1830-1910)

In a grand manner

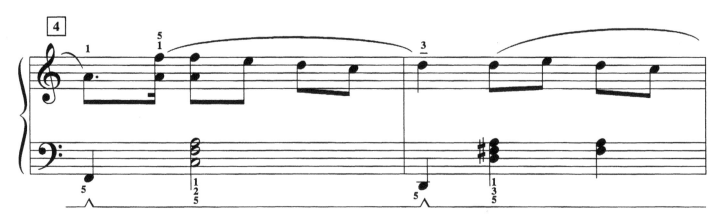

FF1142

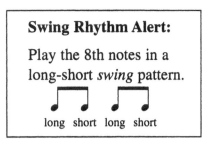
At a "Jazzy" Christmas Party (1915-present)

Bright swing (♫ = ♩³♪)

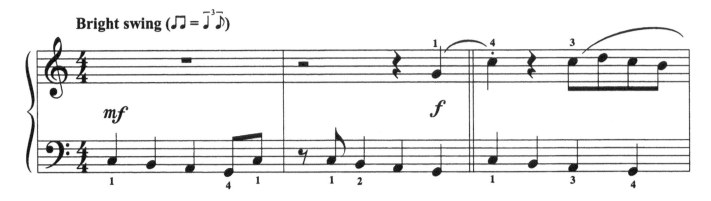

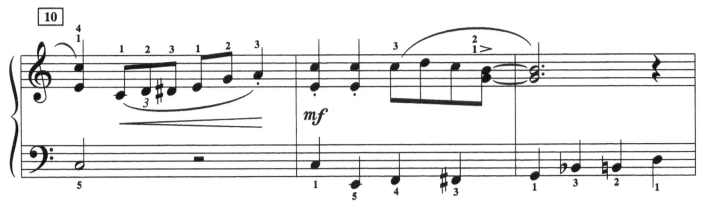

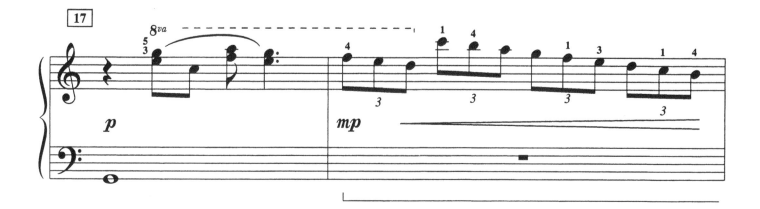

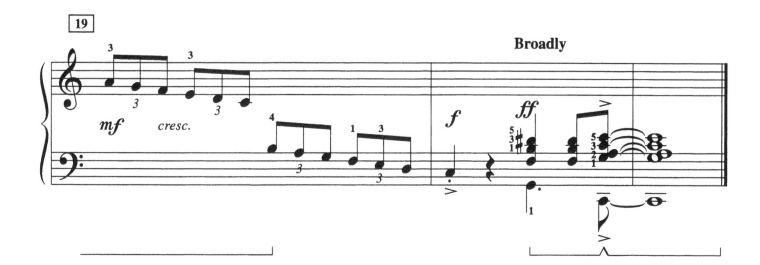

Sightread one "stocking stuffer" a day
while learning *We Wish You a Merry Christmas.*

("variations" for sightreading)

In a Baroque style (Some composers: Bach and Händel)

Extra Credit: Can you transpose to G major? (Don't forget the left hand F♯!)

In a Classical style (Some composers: Mozart and Beethoven)

Extra Credit: Can you transpose to D major?

In a Romantic style (Some composers: Tchaikovsky and Brahms)

Hint: Name the chords in measures 1, 3, 5, and 7 to prepare you for sightreading.

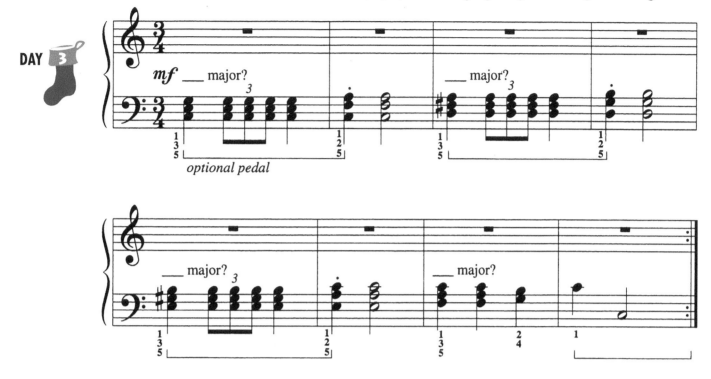

In a Jazz style (Some composers: Louis Armstrong and Glenn Miller)

Which "stocking stuffer" uses an Alberti bass? **Day** _____

Play the Alberti bass pattern several times using these chords:

A minor   D minor   G major   C major

Which musical style is your favorite?

Baroque   Classical

Romantic   Jazz/Contemporary

(circle one)

Fum, Fum, Fum

Key of _____ minor

Spanish Carol

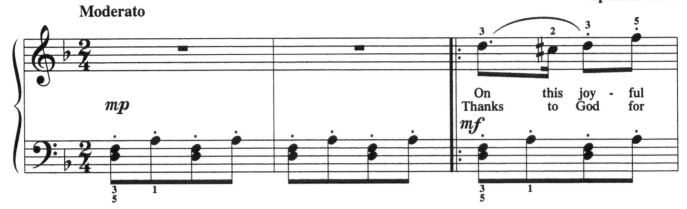

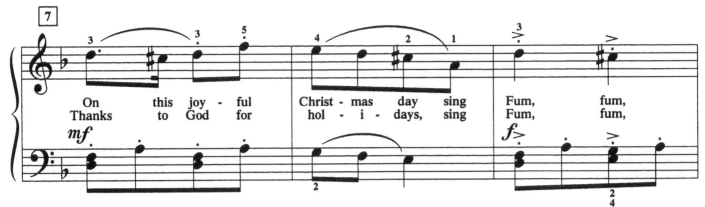

FF1142

day at break of morn. In a man - ger poor and
song of grate - ful praise. Cel - e - brate in song and

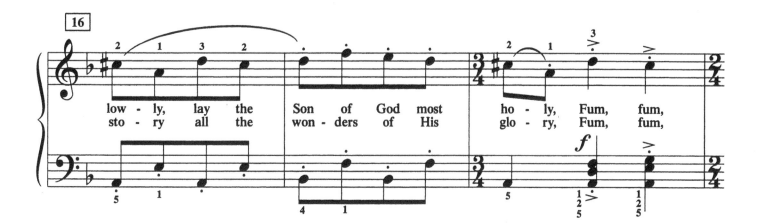

low - ly, lay the Son of God most ho - ly, Fum, fum,
sto - ry all the won - ders of His glo - ry, Fum, fum,

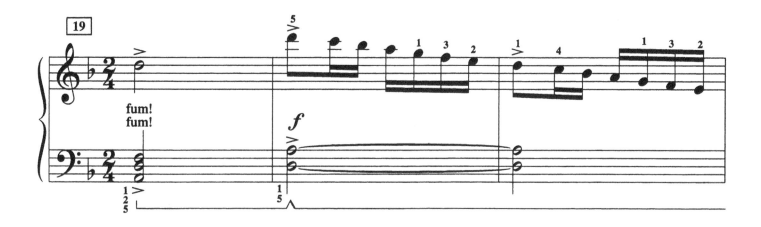

fum!
fum!

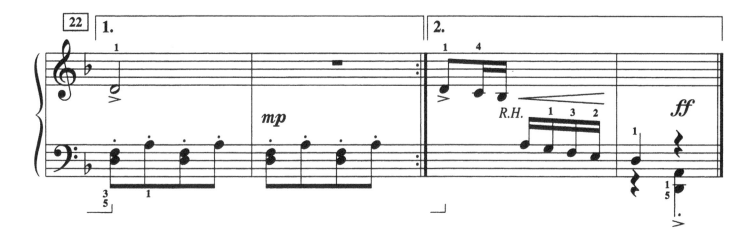

Sightread one "stocking stuffer" a day while learning *Fum, Fum, Fum*. Your teacher may also ask you to transpose.

Circle the stocking after sightreading!

FUM, FUM, FUM STOCKING STUFFERS

("variations" for sightreading)

Can you transpose to E minor?

DAY 1

Can you transpose to A minor?

DAY 2

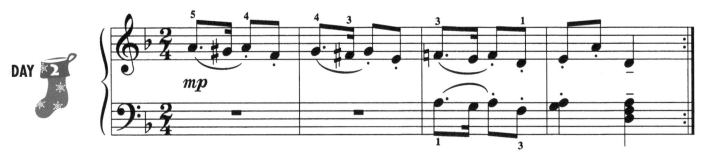

Can you transpose to E major?

DAY 3

DAY 4

What is the opening key of the carol?

_____ minor

DAY 5

In what measure does the carol go to the **relative major** (F major)?

measure _____

In the carol, what form of the minor scale is used at measure twenty?

DAY 6

D natural minor

or

D harmonic minor

(circle one)

FF1142